Love Poems for Michael

by

Joan McNerney

Cyberwit.net
HIG 45 Kaushambi Kunj, Kalindipuram
Allahabad - 211011 (U.P.) India
http://www.cyberwit.net
Tel: +(91) 9415091004 +(91) (532) 2552257
E-mail: info@cyberwit.net

Introduction

Most associate New England with autumn foliage and fierce winters. However four seasons do include bursting springs and boiling summers. Love is year round but let's dwell on spring and summer up north.

Love is its own season, its own country, its own domain. When you have it, you know it. Here's a peek at my love life with a native New Englander who always loved New York and one special New Yorker... me!

Contents

Guess what?

 After this New England
winter, I want to take
off my clothes...so bad.
But could it be cold
here even in summer?

Imagine naked under the
sun. Swimming through
one million lakes. Or
lying on grass...so warm
warm warm.

Maybe count every leaf
on every tree. I've
always wanted to do that.
And stars too!

Would you come with me?
Lots of puritans would
disapprove. Yes they
would. Sometimes their
eyes are like granite.

We could climb those hills.
They'd just say we're
crazy, running out with
no clothes and leave us alone.

Then what would we do?

Almost

As if you could come so swiftly
unnoticed like butterflies tapping
wild flowers with soft yellow wings.

Appearing before me quietly
while morning mist curls through
coolness of mint-green spring.

You walking over roads through
fields where tree shadows make
heavy slants against the sun.

As alive as day...saying my name...
filling me up with the taste of you...
kissing my mouth awake again.

By touch and whisper how we would
imitate long leaves weaving, undulating
and finally surrendering to silence.

Tonight

Chimes tap against our
windowpane. This evening
becomes starry sapphire
as sea gulls rise in
flight over rooftops.

Winds wrapping around
trees tossing leaves.
The court yard is full of
aromas from dinnertime.

Shadows growing longer
each minute. Lights go
on and I wait for you.

Cape Cod

Hearing waves from a distance and
feeling sea breezes brush our faces,
it seemed a century before we
came to the ocean.

So blue and bright to our eyes
its rhythm broke chains of
unremarkable days.

Over cool sand we ran and you picked
three perfect shells which fit
inside each other. Running towards
that moving expanse through
fine spray and splashes.

With clouds cumulus we drifted while
gulls circled the island. Together we
discovered beds of morning glories
climbing soft dunes.

Picnic in the Rain

We wouldn't let the
rain stop us so we had
our picnic in the car.

Crowds evaporated
running with jackets
flung over their heads.

It grew more and more
quiet except for a few
susurrus raindrops.

Us alone drinking wine
walking over meadows
of grass, moist fragrant.
your face so wet
sweet wine.

Last Summer

Golden sunshine spilling
over cathedrals of trees
forest of summer.

Your eyes are oceans of light
beams of light soft beaming
dancing through rivers of memory.

Forest of rivers
drowning in oceans of eyes.
Your eyes when sunset spreads
over sand dunes warm golden.

Stars gliding past heaven
as night explodes in
cathedrals of light.

We bed down together in
forest of memories
your body so strong golden
last summer with you.

Birthday Present

I wanted to bring back the
best gift from the country
for you, just for you.
I wanted to.

Some sky would be nice,
lots of lovely sky with
light fleecy clouds.

So I rushed through
stores and bought the
biggest shiny box and
looked for a perfect bow.

All shades of blue, violet
with red and yellow.
An entire rainbow of
colored ribbons for the
box to put this sky into.

Then on the bus my bow
fell apart. Somebody
stepped on the box. It's
all crushed and dirty.

By the time we got to
the city it was late. Did

my sky fly away?
The box is empty now.

I wanted to bring back the
best gift from the country
for you, just for you.
I wanted to.

Ripples creep over our feet

Should we stand shivering or
dive in? Lose our footprints?

The sun is a giant beach ball.
See it splashing through
waves all red violet blue.

Weaving around this ocean
my legs encircle your waist.
You are so massive and wonderful.

Perhaps we can discover some
great canyons where stars
fell one billion years ago.

I see beams of light in
your hands touching their
cool luminosity now.

Amazed

I am whispering
your name. O Michael
how I love to touch
your sweet neck with
my tongue. Your
name always comes
to my mouth wanting to
hold you kiss only you
with my electric tongue.

How amazing you are
O my dearest Michael
your eyes astonished
speaking so silently
speaking always to me.

Waiting

At the bus station so
I would not walk alone
from the night shift.
How you looked in black night
under a lamp post laughing
after yet another long day.

You wanted to make
me a perfect world.
Always talking about
when we move to Mexico
then I would never
lift another finger.

We savor avocado and
toast, sipping tea.
You whisper sweet nothings.
Our hearts beating together.

Night Waltz

O Michael tonight
I am dreaming of you.

We trace night with
our fingers climbing
ladders of darkness
past the full moon
over silver light into
star light we dance
through air redolent
with lilacs. Your eyes
glow like burning comets
as we waltz over clouds.

O Michael tonight
I dreamed of you and
woke to find you
sleeping at my side.

Shimmering

How I wanted to be
naked under the sun.
Tango all over warm grass,
so warm, warm.

Noontime perfumed berries
and lush grass. Beneath honey
locust through hushed woods
we found this spring,
a secret susurrus disco.

My feet began two-stepping
over slippery pebbles.
Threading soft water, the sun
dresses us in golden sequins.

Your hand reaches for me.

Seasons of Love

Spring Tide

Green I wore green
that night when we
danced how we danced
at the picnic during
   spring
lustrous and green.

Raindrops filling the
air where we danced.
You left whispering
sweet words
   kissing
my eyes closed.

Sliding under green green
waters slipping sliding
over night
   hiding
in nebulae
turning we dance
how we dance through
this wondrous night.

I see you in bright colors

Eating red ripe watermelon
while searching verdant trees
for bluebirds flitting pass us.

Remembering how fields
of brilliant wildflowers
beguiled us as we inhaled
fresh mowed grasses.

You would smile fingering
purple passion leaves.

Your favorite hour when
wide awake you listened
to the sounds of dawn
calling all colors out to play.

We share the calligraphy of
oceans watching orange sunsets
splash through waves.

No one else has ever evoked
such a shining palate as you.

Apple Time

Red yellow brown carpets
of crunchy leaves spread
out to welcome you.

You are coming home to aromas
of cinnamon and me. I've been
waiting so long
to touch you
    feed you
    juicy apples.

Finally you are here.
Red giant stars
growing
our names
glowing
in neons
for eons.

Winter Solstice

Ice blue mountains,
wind swept skies.
There are always these...

And you standing
silent as the sun
burning through
this day.
You are my sun
my heaven on earth.

You bring bright ribbons
handfuls of crystal
to fasten my hair.

Stay with me this
long evening. I will
hide in your arms away
from ice blue winds.
We will be warm together.